WeightWatchers®
seasonal sensations

Over 40 low Point recipes

Edited by Sue Beveridge

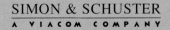

SIMON & SCHUSTER
A VIACOM COMPANY

First published in Great Britain by
Simon & Schuster UK Ltd, 2003
A Viacom Company

All the recipes in this book have been published previously by Weight Watchers.

Simon & Schuster UK Ltd
Africa House
64–78 Kingsway
London
WC2B 6AH

Photography and styling by Steve Baxter
Food preparation by Carol Tennant

Design by Jane Humphrey
Typesetting by Stylize Digital Artwork
Printed and bound in Italy / Hong Kong / Singapore

Weight Watchers Publications Manager: Corrina Griffin
Weight Watchers Publications Executives: Lucy Davidson, Mandy Spittle
Weight Watchers Publications Assistant: Nina Bhogal

A CIP catalogue for this book is available from the British Library

ISBN 0 74323 909 1

Pictured on the front cover: Pork and honey stir fry (page 9); Roly pavlova (page 31); Root and orange soup (page 34); Orange and lemon cheesecake (page 16)

Pictured on the back cover: Bread and butter pudding (page 59)

All fruits, vegetables and eggs are medium size unless otherwise stated. Teaspoons (5 ml) and tablespoons (15 ml) are level.

(v) denotes a vegetarian recipe and assumes vegetarian cheese and free range eggs are used. Virtually fat free fromage frais and low fat crème fraiche may contain traces of gelatine so they are not always vegetarian: please check the labels.

Recipe timings are approximate and meant to be guidelines. Please note that the preparation time includes all the steps up to and following the main cooking time(s).

POINTS You'll find this easy to read logo on every recipe throughout the book. The logo represents the number of Points per serving each recipe contains. The easy to use Points system is designed to help you eat what you want, when you want – as long as you stay within your Points allowance – giving you the freedom to enjoy the food you love.

contents

One of the keys to creating tasty meals is to use good quality, seasonal produce. That way, you'll know that each ingredient is in peak condition and will have maximum flavour. So here is a collection of recipes, sorted into seasonal chapters, to make it easier for you to do just that. In addition, every recipe is Pointed so that you can easily fit it into your daily Points when following the **Time To Eat**™ Programme. As usual, there is also all the information you'll need regarding timings and freezing. You'll find many family favourites as well as lots of new ideas to try – all of them are lower in Points than their traditional recipe counterparts.

Spring brings you Salmon and Asparagus Supreme and Hot Cross Buns (pages 11 and 18), summer has some tasty barbecue ideas (Chilli Beef Burgers, page 22, and Chicken Kebabs, page 23) as well as a wonderful pavlova with a twist – Roly Pavlova (page 31)! Autumn just had to include a warming Apple Pie (page 44). It also has a tasty Fish Pie with Herby Mash (page 38). Winter, of course, includes Christmas Pudding and Brandy Sauce (page 61) along with a satisfying beef casserole – which wouldn't be the same without dumplings, so you can be sure you'll find them in Beef in Ale with Dumplings (page 50). Over half of the recipes are vegetarian. You'll also find that the recipes produce a variety of servings from one to sixteen – so however many you are cooking for, you're sure to find a recipe to suit.

Using seasonal ingredients also means that they're often available from local producers. So by choosing recipes to suit the seasons, you are also helping to reduce the number of miles our food travels, and therefore helping the environment too. Truly guilt free food in every respect!

spring
recipes

serves: **4**   preparation: **10** mins   cooking: **30** mins

14 POINTS PER RECIPE

- **25 g (1 oz) polyunsaturated margarine**
- **1 large onion, chopped**
- **600 ml (20 fl oz) vegetable stock**
- **25 g (1 oz) fresh parsley**
- **200 g bag of watercress**
- **2 tablespoons cornflour**
- **425 ml (15 fl oz) skimmed milk**
- **200 g (7 oz) low fat soft cheese**
- **salt and freshly ground black pepper**
- **4 tablespoons low fat plain yogurt, to garnish**

Creamy watercress soup

1 Melt the margarine in a large saucepan and fry the onion gently over a low heat for about 3 minutes, until softened but not brown.

2 Pour in the stock, add the parsley (including the stems) and all but a few sprigs of watercress. You don't need to chop these as you will be blending them later. Bring to the boil, reduce the heat, cover the pan and simmer for 15–20 minutes.

3 Remove from the heat and use a blender (or a food processor) to liquidise everything to a smooth consistency. Clean the pan.

4 Mix the cornflour with 3–4 tablespoons of the milk. Pour the soup back into the pan and return to the heat. Add the cornflour paste to the soup and bring to the boil, stirring continuously until the soup has thickened. Simmer for about 2 minutes.

5 Add the soft cheese and remaining milk. Gently heat through until well combined. Season to taste and ladle into four warmed bowls. Top each bowlful with a tablespoon of yogurt and some of the reserved watercress.

Freezing recommended

Mushroom and chilli pâté

3 POINTS PER RECIPE

1 Place all the ingredients in a large saucepan. Stir gently while bringing to a medium heat. Cover the pan with a tight fitting lid and leave to cook on a gentle heat for 10 minutes.

2 Remove the lid, turn the heat up and stir continuously for 2–3 minutes or until all the juices have dried up.

3 Check the seasoning and then spoon into four small dishes, or one larger one. Cover with clingfilm and chill for at least 1 hour before serving.

Freezing not recommended

- **200 g (7 oz) button mushrooms, chopped finely**
- **1 small onion, chopped finely**
- **1 large red chilli, de-seeded and chopped finely**
- **2 tablespoons half fat crème fraîche**
- **salt and freshly ground black pepper**

Pork and honey stir fry

1 Cook the noodles according to the packet instructions.

2 Meanwhile, heat a wok or large frying pan. Spray with the low fat cooking spray, then add the sesame oil. Add the garlic and pork and stir fry over a high heat for 4 minutes.

3 Add the honey, soy sauce and ginger. Cook for a further 2 minutes.

4 Drain the noodles, add the vegetables and cooked noodles to the pork and toss together. Cook for a further minute or two then serve immediately.

Freezing not recommended

5 POINTS

10 POINTS PER RECIPE

- **100 g (3½ oz) fine egg noodles**
- **low fat cooking spray**
- **½ teaspoon sesame oil**
- **1 garlic clove, sliced finely**
- **200 g (7 oz) pork tenderloin, sliced thinly**
- **½ tablespoon honey**
- **2 tablespoons soy sauce**
- **1 cm (½ inch) fresh root ginger, sliced into matchsticks**
- **50 g (1¾ oz) mange tout, sliced into thin strips**
- **1 carrot, sliced into matchsticks**
- **50 g (1¾ oz) baby spinach**
- **½ bunch of spring onions, shredded**

serves: **1**   preparation + cooking: **15** mins

2½ POINTS PER RECIPE

- **low fat cooking spray**
- **100 g (3½ oz) turkey breast strips**
- **50 g (1¾ oz) mange tout, trimmed**
- **1 spring onion, sliced**
- **½ tablespoon honey**
- **1 tablespoon lemon juice**
- **6 fresh basil leaves, torn**
- **½ teaspoon sesame seeds**
- **salt and freshly ground black pepper**

Lemon glazed turkey

1 Spray a large frying pan with low fat cooking spray and stir fry the turkey strips for 3–4 minutes until the meat is sealed and starting to brown.

2 Add the mange tout and spring onion. Stir fry for a further 3–4 minutes.

3 Add the honey, lemon juice, basil and sesame seeds. Season to taste.

4 Let the juices boil and toss the mixture well to coat the turkey in the glaze that is forming. Serve immediately.

Freezing not recommended

Salmon and asparagus supreme

1 Preheat the oven to Gas Mark 5/190°C/fan oven 170°C.

2 Cook the leeks and courgettes for 5 minutes in lightly salted boiling water. In another saucepan, cook the asparagus, in lightly salted boiling water for the same amount of time. Drain the vegetables and leave to cool.

3 Divide the smoked salmon into six pieces and wrap one piece around each asparagus spear.

4 Season the leeks and courgettes and put half of them into a shallow ovenproof dish. Place the wrapped asparagus on top and cover with the remaining vegetables.

5 Put the low fat spread, cornflour, milk and a tablespoon of the parmesan cheese into a saucepan. Heat gently until thickened, stirring constantly with a small whisk. Season and then pour over the vegetables and salmon. Sprinkle the other tablespoon of parmesan cheese over the top and bake for 25–30 minutes, until hot and golden.

Freezing recommended

9 POINTS PER RECIPE

- **2 large leeks, sliced**
- **2 large courgettes, sliced**
- **6 large (or 12 small) asparagus spears, trimmed**
- **125 g (4½ oz) smoked salmon**
- **2 teaspoons low fat spread**
- **1 tablespoon cornflour**
- **200 ml (7 fl oz) skimmed milk**
- **2 tablespoons freshly grated parmesan cheese**
- **salt and freshly ground black pepper**

5½ POINTS PER RECIPE

- **2 x 175 g (6 oz) cod steaks**
- **finely grated zest and juice of ½ lemon**
- **1 teaspoon olive oil**
- **3 tablespoons chopped fresh herbs, such as dill, chives or parsley**
- **salt and freshly ground black pepper**

Grilled cod with spring herbs

1 Preheat the grill to medium hot. Rinse the cod steaks and pat them dry with kitchen paper. Line a grill pan with foil and place the steaks on it.

2 Mix together the lemon zest, lemon juice, olive oil, herbs and seasoning. Spoon half the mixture over one side of the fish and grill for 2−3 minutes.

3 Turn the fish over and spoon over the remaining herb mixture. Grill for a further 2−3 minutes or until cooked through. Serve at once.

Freezing not recommended

Spring vegetable stew

1 Put the potatoes into a saucepan with the stock and bring to the boil. Reduce the heat, cover, and simmer for 10 minutes.

2 Add the carrots and simmer for another 5 minutes.

3 Add the pesto sauce, garlic and the remaining vegetables to the pan. Cover and bring back to the boil for a further 5 minutes. Season to taste and sprinkle with the basil.

Freezing not recommended

8½ POINTS PER RECIPE

- **400 g (14 oz) new potatoes**
- **600 ml (20 fl oz) hot vegetable stock**
- **200 g (7 oz) baby carrots, quartered lengthways**
- **2 tablespoons pesto sauce**
- **2 garlic cloves, sliced**
- **1 bunch of spring onions, chopped**
- **200 g (7 oz) sugar snap peas**
- **200 g (7 oz) green beans, halved**
- **100 g (3½ oz) frozen petits pois**
- **100 g (3½ oz) frozen broad beans**
- **salt and freshly ground black pepper**
- **chopped fresh basil, to garnish**

4½ POINTS

18½ POINTS PER RECIPE

- **1 tablespoon olive oil**
- **1 onion, chopped**
- **2 garlic cloves, crushed**
- **250 g (9 oz) risotto rice**
- **3 tablespoons dry white wine**
- **1 litre (1¾ pints) hot vegetable stock**
- **250 g (9 oz) various fresh No Point tender vegetables, cut into bite size pieces, e.g. baby carrots, baby corn, button mushrooms or asparagus**
- **salt and freshly ground black pepper**
- **25 g (1 oz) freshly grated parmesan cheese, to serve**

Risotto primavera

1 Heat the oil on a medium heat in a large saucepan and gently sauté the onion and garlic for 5 minutes.

2 Stir in the rice and cook for 1 minute. Then add the wine and stir until it is absorbed.

3 Pour in a quarter of the hot stock and stir frequently for about 3 minutes until it is absorbed.

4 Add any firm vegetables such as carrots. Add the remaining stock a ladle at a time, stirring frequently until it is absorbed before adding the next ladleful. As you add the stock, add the other vegetables, leaving the most tender (such as asparagus) until the last 5 minutes. It will take 25–30 minutes to add all the stock, by which time the rice should be cooked. If the rice still seems too firm, add a little boiling water and stir until absorbed.

5 Season well and serve as soon as it's ready, topped with the parmesan cheese.

Freezing not recommended

Rhubarb and ginger crumble

1 Put the rhubarb into a saucepan with the jam, caster sugar, orange juice and ginger. Cook gently for 5–10 minutes until tender. Preheat the oven to Gas Mark 4/180°C/fan oven 160°C.

2 Mix the cornflour with a little cold water to make a paste and then stir this into the rhubarb. Cook until the juices thicken. Transfer the mixture to a shallow ovenproof dish.

3 To make the crumble topping, mix together the oats, breadcrumbs, sugar, honey and cinnamon. Scatter over the rhubarb and spray several times with the low fat cooking spray. Bake for 20–25 minutes, until the topping is golden and crunchy.

Freezing recommended

16 POINTS PER RECIPE

- **450 g (1 lb) rhubarb, chopped into 2 cm (¾ inch) pieces**
- **3 tablespoons reduced sugar strawberry jam**
- **50 g (1¾ oz) caster sugar**
- **juice of 1 orange**
- **1 teaspoon ground ginger**
- **1 tablespoon cornflour**
  For the crumble topping
- **75 g (2¾ oz) porridge oats**
- **50 g (1¾ oz) fresh white breadcrumbs**
- **25 g (1 oz) demerara sugar**
- **4 tablespoons honey, warmed**
- **½ teaspoon ground cinnamon**
- **low fat cooking spray**

4
POINTS

32 POINTS PER RECIPE

- **150 g (5½ oz) reduced fat digestive biscuits**
- **50 g (1¾ oz) low fat spread**
- **2 teaspoons golden syrup**
  For the filling
- **200 g (7 oz) low fat soft cheese**
- **50 g (1¾ oz) fructose**
- **grated zest and juice of 1 lemon**
- **grated zest and juice of 1 orange**
- **11g sachet of gelatine**
- **2 x 150 g cartons of low fat orange or lemon flavoured yogurt**
- **1 egg white**
- **2 oranges, peeled and segmented, to decorate**

Orange and lemon cheesecake

1 Put the biscuits in a plastic bag and crush them using a rolling pin. In a saucepan, melt the low fat spread and golden syrup together then thoroughly mix in the biscuit crumbs. Press this mixture firmly into the base of a 20 cm (8 inch) loose bottomed springform tin. Chill while you prepare the topping.

2 Beat together the soft cheese, fructose, lemon zest, lemon juice and orange zest.

3 Place the orange juice in a small heatproof bowl, sprinkle the gelatine over it and leave to stand for 5 minutes, until it becomes spongy. Then place it over a pan of gently simmering water and heat until clear and the gelatine has completely dissolved. Allow to cool for 5 minutes.

4 Beat the gelatine into the soft cheese mixture with the yogurt. Whisk the egg white until it forms soft peaks and fold in. Spoon over the biscuit base, level the top and leave to chill for at least 3 hours.

5 To serve, carefully remove from the tin onto a serving plate and arrange the orange segments around the edge.

Freezing recommended (undecorated)

40½ POINTS PER RECIPE

- low fat cooking spray
- 350 g (12 oz) plain flour plus 30 g (1¼ oz) for dusting
- ½ teaspoon caster sugar
- 150 ml (5 fl oz) warm water
- 1 tablespoon dried yeast
- 100 g (3½ oz) wholemeal flour
- 1 teaspoon salt
- 1 teaspoon ground cinnamon
- 1 teaspoon ground nutmeg
- 50 g (1¾ oz) caster sugar
- 75 g (2¾ oz) currants
- 50 g (1¾ oz) chopped mixed peel
- 4 tablespoons skimmed milk, warmed
- 1 egg, beaten
- 50 g (1¾ oz) polyunsaturated margarine, melted

Hot cross buns

1 Spray two baking trays with low fat cooking spray and lightly dust them with a little of the extra plain flour.

2 In a bowl, dissolve the caster sugar in the warm water. Sprinkle in the dried yeast. Leave for 5 minutes in a warm place to froth.

3 Meanwhile, sift the flours, salt, cinnamon and nutmeg into a mixing bowl, then stir in the remaining sugar, currants and mixed peel. Make a well in the centre and pour in the frothy yeast mixture, 3 tablespoons of the warm milk, the egg and the melted margarine. Mix together with a wooden spoon and then knead with your hands for about 5 minutes. Leave, covered, in a warm place to rise for an hour, or until the dough has doubled in size.

4 Turn the risen dough out on to a work surface dusted with flour and knead for a couple of minutes. Shape the dough into 16 rounds and space them out well on the baking trays. Mark each with a cross using a sharp knife. Cover and leave to rise again for 20 minutes. Preheat the oven to Gas Mark 7/220°C/fan oven 200°C.

5 Gently brush the buns with the last tablespoon of skimmed milk to glaze, and bake for 15 minutes. Once baked, remove the buns from the baking trays and leave to cool on a wire rack.

Freezing recommended

summer
recipes

serves: **6**   preparation: **15** mins + **10** mins soaking + **3** hrs chilling

7 POINTS PER RECIPE

- **2 medium slices of slightly stale bread, crusts removed**
- **1 kg (2 lb 4 oz) ripe tomatoes, peeled and halved**
- **½ cucumber, cut into chunks**
- **1 small red onion, cut into chunks**
- **2 garlic cloves**
- **1 red or green pepper, de-seeded and cut into chunks**
- **2 tablespoons olive oil**
- **2 tablespoons white wine vinegar**
- **½ small bunch of fresh parsley**
- **a handful of fresh basil leaves**
- **salt and freshly ground black pepper**
  To serve
- **fresh basil leaves**
- **ice cubes**

Gazpacho

1 Soak the bread in water for 10 minutes. Then squeeze it a little and blend in a food processor with all the remaining ingredients. Taste and season. (If you do not have a food processor, finely chop all the vegetables, herbs and bread and mix with all the other ingredients for a slightly chunkier version.)

2 Empty into a container and chill for 2–3 hours.

3 Serve chilled, with the ice cubes and fresh basil leaves.

Freezing not recommended

Warm goat's cheese salad

 V

1 Preheat the grill to high. Cut the baguette into 18 diagonal slices and spread each with a little goat's cheese. Place these under the grill for a few minutes or until they begin to brown at the edges.

2 Meanwhile, place the salad in a bowl and put all the vinaigrette ingredients into a screw top jar. Put on the lid and shake well. Pour over the salad and toss together.

3 Divide the dressed salad between six plates. Top each with three of the goat's cheese croûtons and serve immediately as a starter.

Freezing not recommended

3 POINTS

18½ POINTS PER RECIPE

- **200 g (7 oz) baguette**
- **100 g (3½ oz) goat's cheese (e.g. crottin)**
- **200 g (7 oz) bag of mixed herb and baby salad leaves**
  For the vinaigrette
- **1 tablespoon balsamic vinegar**
- **2 teaspoons wholegrain mustard**
- **2 tablespoons very low fat, plain fromage frais**
- **salt and freshly ground black pepper**

makes: **4** burgers   preparation: **5** mins   cooking: **15** mins

22 POINTS PER RECIPE

- **1 small onion, chopped finely**
- **1 tablespoon Worcestershire sauce**
- **350 g (12 oz) extra lean minced beef**
- **1 pickled gherkin, chopped finely**
- **1 teaspoon dried chilli flakes**
- **1 egg, beaten**
- **4 medium burger buns, halved**
- **1 beef tomato, sliced thinly**
- **a few lettuce leaves, to garnish**

Chilli beef burgers

1 Place the onion in a small pan with 2 tablespoons of water and the Worcestershire sauce. Cover and cook gently for 2 to 3 minutes until softened. Preheat the grill to medium, or ensure your barbecue is ready.

2 Drain the onion thoroughly and place in a mixing bowl. Add the beef, gherkin, chilli flakes and as much of the egg as you need to bind the ingredients together. Mix well.

3 Divide the mixture into four and mould into evenly sized burgers. Grill or barbecue for 5 minutes on each side or until the burgers are cooked through. If desired, you may also wish to toast the burger buns at this stage.

4 Serve the burgers in the burger buns, with the tomato slices, garnished with the lettuce leaves.

Freezing recommended for the burgers only

Chicken kebabs

1 Preheat the grill to medium, or ensure your barbecue is ready. Place all the marinade ingredients in a screw top jar and shake well to mix.

2 Thread pieces of chicken, onion, pepper, bay leaves and lemon wedges, alternately, on to four skewers. Put some marinade to one side for serving, and pour the rest into a separate bowl and use to brush the kebabs. (This ensures no raw chicken juices get into your reserved marinade.)

3 Grill or barbecue for about 10 minutes until golden and cooked through, turning at least once. Meanwhile, warm the pitta breads under the grill or at the edge of the barbecue rack.

4 Remove everything from the skewers and place it all into the warm pitta breads, with the lettuce, tomato slices and the remaining marinade. Serve immediately.

Freezing not recommended

8 ½ POINTS PER RECIPE

- **200 g (7 oz) skinless, boneless chicken breasts, cut into chunks**
- **2 red onions, cut into wedges**
- **2 differently coloured peppers, de-seeded and cut into squares**
- **4 bay leaves**
- **½ lemon, cut into wedges**
- **2 medium pitta breads**
- **¼ Iceberg lettuce, shredded**
- **4 tomatoes, sliced**
  For the marinade
- **1 garlic clove, crushed**
- **1 tablespoon low fat plain yogurt**
- **½ tablespoon honey**
- **½ tablespoon soy sauce**
- **1 tablespoon red wine vinegar or lemon juice**

serves: **4**   preparation: **10** mins   cooking: **35** mins

6
POINTS

24 POINTS PER RECIPE

- low fat cooking spray
- 2 medium skinless, boneless chicken breasts, cut into strips
- 1 onion, chopped
- 1 red pepper, de-seeded and chopped
- 3 garlic cloves, crushed
- 3 ripe tomatoes, chopped
- a large pinch of saffron strands
- 2 teaspoons paprika
- 2 tablespoons chopped fresh thyme
- 250 g (9 oz) paella rice
- 600 ml (20 fl oz) chicken stock
- 400 g (14 oz) frozen seafood, defrosted
- 125 g (4½ oz) frozen peas
- salt and freshly ground black pepper
- lemon wedges, to serve

Paella

1 Spray a large pan with the cooking spray and stir fry the chicken strips for 5 minutes. Remove the chicken from the pan and leave to one side.

2 Spray the pan again with the cooking spray. Add the onion, red pepper and garlic to the pan. Stir fry for 3–4 minutes or until softened. Add the tomatoes, saffron, paprika and thyme, then season with salt and pepper. Cook for a further 2 minutes.

3 Add the rice and stir well until mixed, then add the stock. Bring to a gentle simmer and cook uncovered for 10 minutes.

4 Add the chicken and gently simmer, uncovered, for a further 10 minutes without stirring. Lastly, add the seafood and the peas. Stir briefly to mix, bring back to simmering point and cook for a final 5 minutes (or until the rice is cooked).

5 Check the seasoning and serve with the lemon wedges.

Freezing not recommended

serves: **1**   preparation + cooking: **15** mins

3½ POINTS PER RECIPE

- **150 g (5½ oz) fresh tuna steak**
- **½ tablespoon pesto sauce**
- **lemon wedges, to serve**
  For the salsa
- **75 g (2¾ oz) cherry tomatoes, chopped finely**
- **½ small red onion, chopped finely**
- **a handful of fresh basil leaves, torn**
- **1 teaspoon balsamic vinegar**
- **½ teaspoon olive oil**
- **salt and freshly ground black pepper**

Pesto tuna with tomato salsa

1 Preheat the grill to medium and line the grill pan with foil. Mix all the salsa ingredients in a bowl and put to one side.

2 Place the tuna steak on the foil and spread half of the pesto sauce on top. Grill for 4 minutes. Turn the tuna over, spread on the remaining pesto and grill for another 4 minutes or until cooked through.

3 Serve immediately with the salsa and lemon wedges.

Freezing not recommended

Summer spaghetti

1 Bring a large pan of lightly salted water to the boil and cook the spaghetti until tender.

2 Meanwhile, heat the olive oil in a large frying pan and cook the shallots until softened, but not brown. Add the lemon zest, lemon juice and stock. Allow it to bubble for 2 minutes.

3 Drain the spaghetti, return it to the pan and toss with the lemon sauce, tomatoes, mozzarella, parmesan and seasoning. Heat through for a minute or two and then pile on to warm plates to serve.

Freezing not recommended

17 POINTS PER RECIPE

- **125 g (4½ oz) spaghetti**
- **1 teaspoon olive oil**
- **2 shallots, chopped finely**
- **finely grated zest of 1 lemon**
- **2 tablespoons fresh lemon juice**
- **4 tablespoons vegetable stock**
- **225 g (8 oz) cherry tomatoes, halved**
- **100 g (3½ oz) mozzarella light cheese, cubed**
- **2 tablespoons freshly grated parmesan cheese**
- **salt and freshly ground black pepper**

serves: **4**   preparation: **15** mins   cooking: **25** mins

3½ POINTS

13 POINTS PER RECIPE

- low fat cooking spray
- 1 small onion, chopped finely
- 1 garlic clove, crushed
- 1 teaspoon ground coriander
- 1 teaspoon ground cumin
- ½ teaspoon chilli flakes
- 425 g can of chick peas, drained
- 1 small egg
- 25 g (1 oz) wholemeal breadcrumbs
- 3 tablespoons chopped fresh coriander
- salt and freshly ground black pepper
- shredded lettuce, to serve
  For the dressing
- 150 ml (5 fl oz) low fat plain yogurt
- 2 tablespoons mint jelly
- ½ cucumber, diced finely

Chick pea falafel

1 Preheat the oven to Gas Mark 5/190°C/fan oven 170°C. Spray a non stick frying pan with the low fat cooking spray. Gently cook the onion and garlic until softened but not brown. Stir in the ground coriander, cumin and chilli flakes. Cook for a minute and then remove from the heat.

2 Place in a food processor with the chick peas, egg, breadcrumbs, seasoning and fresh coriander.

3 Blend until well combined and then, using your hands and a dessertspoon, shape the mixture into 16 small balls. Place them on to a non stick baking sheet and cook for 20 minutes.

4 To make the dressing, mix the yogurt and mint jelly together and then stir in the cucumber. Season to taste.

5 Serve the falafel on a bed of shredded lettuce, drizzled with the mint and cucumber dressing.

Freezing recommended for the falafel

Summer pudding

 V

1 Place the fruit in a saucepan with the sugar and cook gently for 10 minutes, or until the fruit is just tender.

2 Cut a circle of bread to fit into the bottom of an 850 ml (1 ½ pint) pudding basin and another the same size as the top.

3 Cut the remaining bread slices in half lengthways. Arrange these, and the smaller circle of bread neatly around the inside of the bowl so that it is completely covered. Overlap slightly at the joins.

4 Drain the fruit, reserving the juices, and put the fruit into the bread lined bowl. Sprinkle the rose water over the fruit (if using) and pour over most of the reserved juice, leaving a few tablespoons to one side. Cover the top with the larger circle of bread. Place a small saucer on top so that it fits just inside the bowl and lies directly on top of the bread. Weigh the saucer down with something heavy such as a large can or a clean stone. Leave overnight in the fridge.

5 To serve, remove the weight and the saucer and turn out on to a plate (gently loosening the edges of the bread with a palette knife if necessary). Use the reserved juices to colour any bread that's still white or use as a sauce to serve with the pudding.

Freezing not recommended

17 POINTS PER RECIPE

- **500 g bag of mixed frozen summer berries, defrosted**
- **100 g (3½ oz) caster sugar**
- **8 medium slices of white bread, crusts removed**
- **2 teaspoons rose water (optional)**

Roly pavlova

 (V)

1 Preheat the oven to Gas Mark 2/150°C/fan oven 130°C. Line a 23 x 33 cm (9 x 13 inch) Swiss roll tin with baking parchment.

2 Blend together the vanilla essence, vinegar and cornflour.

3 Whisk the egg whites in a grease free bowl until stiff peaks form. Whisk in a third of the cornflour mixture and a third of the caster sugar. Repeat twice more, until all the cornflour and sugar is well incorporated and the mixture is thick and glossy.

4 Spoon the meringue on to the prepared tin and level the surface. Bake for 45 minutes, then turn off the oven and leave the meringue in the oven for a further 15 minutes.

5 Carefully turn out the meringue on to a large piece of greaseproof paper and peel off the backing paper. Allow to cool completely.

6 Just before serving, spread the crème fraîche over the meringue and sprinkle with the fruit. Gently roll up as you would a Swiss roll and place on a serving plate. Don't worry if the meringue cracks in places, it will still look and taste great when sliced and served!

Freezing not recommended

3 POINTS

23½ POINTS PER RECIPE

- **1 teaspoon vanilla essence**
- **1 teaspoon vinegar**
- **1 teaspoon cornflour**
- **4 egg whites**
- **200 g (7 oz) caster sugar**
- **200 ml (7 fl oz) half fat crème fraîche**
- **500 g bag of mixed frozen summer fruits, defrosted and drained**

serves: **12**   preparation: **15** mins + **15** mins cooling   cooking: **30** mins

27 POINTS PER RECIPE

- low fat cooking spray
- 110 g (4 oz) polenta, plus 2 teaspoons extra to dust
- 110 g (4 oz) plain flour
- 1½ teaspoons baking powder
- 2 large eggs, plus 3 large egg whites
- 175 g (6 oz) caster sugar
- finely grated zest and juice of 2 lemons
- 1 teaspoon vanilla extract
- 200 ml (7 fl oz) low fat plain yogurt
- 1 teaspoon icing sugar, for dusting

Lemon polenta cake

1 Preheat the oven to Gas Mark 4/180°C/fan oven 160°C. Spray the base of a 25 cm (10 inch) springform cake tin with the low fat cooking spray. Dust the tin with a little polenta.

2 Sift the flour and baking powder together into a bowl and stir in the polenta.

3 In a separate bowl, whisk the whole eggs, egg whites and sugar together until the mixture is pale and thick.

4 Add the polenta mixture, lemon zest and juice, vanilla and yogurt to the egg mixture. Carefully fold together using a large metal spoon.

5 Spoon the mixture into the prepared tin and bake for 30 minutes.

6 Release the sides of the tin and leave the cake to cool for 15 minutes or so. When ready to serve, transfer to a plate and dust with icing sugar – it's best served slightly warm.

Freezing not recommended

autumn
recipes

serves: **6**   preparation: **15** mins   cooking: **20** mins

½ POINT PER RECIPE

- **500 g (1 lb 2 oz) carrots, sliced**
- **1 small swede, diced**
- **2 red onions, chopped**
- **1 garlic clove, crushed**
- **1.5 litres (2¾ pints) hot vegetable stock**
- **1 tablespoon tomato purée**
- **1 tablespoon balsamic vinegar**
- **finely grated zest and juice of 1 orange**
- **2 tablespoons chopped fresh parsley or chives, plus extra to garnish**
- **salt and freshly ground black pepper**

Root and orange soup

1 Put the carrots, swede, onions, garlic, stock, tomato purée and balsamic vinegar into a large saucepan and stir well. Bring up to the boil and then simmer gently for 15–20 minutes, or until the vegetables are tender.

2 Leave the soup chunky, or liquidise it in a food processor for a smoother consistency. Stir in the orange zest and juice, with the parsley or chives, and season to taste. Serve in warmed bowls, garnished with the extra herbs.

Freezing recommended

serves: **4**   preparation: **15** mins   cooking: **1¼** hrs

11 POINTS PER RECIPE

- **low fat cooking spray**
- **600 g (1 lb 5 oz) onions, sliced very finely**
- **1 teaspoon caster sugar**
- **1 tablespoon plain flour**
- **1.5 litres (2¾ pints) hot vegetable stock**
- **150 ml (5 fl oz) white wine**
- **salt and freshly ground black pepper**
  To serve
- **8 x 2.5 cm (1 inch) slices of baguette**
- **50 g (1¾ oz) grated half fat mature Cheddar cheese**

French onion soup

1 Heat a large non stick saucepan and spray with the low fat cooking spray. Then add the onions and gently stir fry for 5 minutes, until softened.

2 Season and cover with a piece of baking parchment tucked down the sides of the pan. Cover with a lid and leave the onions to sweat on the lowest possible heat for 15 minutes. Shake the pan occasionally to make sure the mixture does not stick.

3 Remove the lid and the paper and stir well to get any caramelised onions off the bottom of the pan. Sprinkle with the sugar and flour. Cook for a few minutes, stirring.

4 Add the stock and the wine. Bring to the boil. Reduce the heat and simmer, uncovered, for 45 minutes.

5 Just before serving, preheat the grill to high. Check the seasoning then pour the soup into four warmed flameproof bowls. Float two slices of bread on the top of each bowlful and sprinkle with the grated cheese. Grill for 1–2 minutes, until the cheese is bubbling and golden, and then serve immediately.

Freezing not recommended

Chicken casserole

1 Preheat the oven to Gas Mark 4/180°C/fan oven 160°C.

2 Spray a large flameproof casserole dish with the cooking spray and sauté the onion, celery, carrot and leek for about 5 minutes, until softened.

3 Add the chicken to the dish and cook until it is sealed on all sides. Add the wine and let it bubble briefly, then add the stock, herbs and seasoning.

4 Place the lid on the casserole dish and transfer it to the oven and cook for 45 minutes.

5 Blend the cornflour with 3 tablespoons of cold water to make a paste. Add it to the casserole, mix well and then return it to the oven for a further 5 minutes.

6 Check the seasoning and serve on warmed plates.

Freezing recommended

$5\frac{1}{2}$
POINTS

10½ POINTS PER RECIPE

- **low fat cooking spray**
- **1 large onion, sliced**
- **2 celery sticks, sliced**
- **1 carrot, sliced**
- **1 leek, sliced**
- **225 g (8 oz) skinless boneless chicken thighs, cut into large chunks**
- **75 ml (3 fl oz) dry white wine**
- **150 ml (5 fl oz) chicken stock**
- **1 teaspoon dried mixed herbs**
- **½ tablespoon cornflour**
- **salt and freshly ground black pepper**

serves: **4**   preparation: **25** mins   cooking: **35** mins

15 POINTS PER RECIPE

- **450 g (1 lb) potatoes, peeled and quartered**
- **75 g (2¾ oz) low fat soft cheese**
- **150 ml (5 fl oz) skimmed milk, plus 3 tablespoons for mashing**
- **4 tablespoons chopped fresh parsley**
- **225 g (8 oz) leeks, sliced thinly**
- **50 g (1¾ oz) frozen peas**
- **2 tablespoons cornflour**
- **450 g (1 lb) smoked haddock fillets**
- **2 tablespoons dry white wine**
- **salt and freshly ground black pepper**

Fish pie with herby mash

1 Preheat the oven to Gas Mark 5/190°C/fan oven 170°C. Cook the potatoes in lightly salted, boiling water until tender. When cooked, drain and mash the potatoes with the soft cheese, the 3 tablespoons of milk, parsley and seasoning.

2 Meanwhile, cook the leeks in boiling water for 5 minutes, add the peas and then cook for a further 2 minutes. Drain thoroughly.

3 Mix the cornflour with a little of the remaining milk to form a thin paste. Heat the rest of the milk until boiling and then mix in the cornflour paste. Stir well and cook until thickened.

4 Remove any skin from the fish and cut into bite size chunks. Place in a pan, pour over the wine and steam the fish for 5 minutes, shaking the pan occasionally.

5 Add the white sauce, cooked leeks and peas and stir well. Spoon this into a shallow ovenproof dish and top with the herby mash mixture. Bake for 25 minutes, until piping hot and lightly browned on top.

Freezing recommended

Cod and leek parcel

1 Preheat the oven to Gas Mark 4/180°C/fan oven 160°C. Cut a piece of baking parchment about 30 cm (12 inches) square and place the fish in the centre.

2 Cover with the shredded leeks and sprinkle over the lemon zest, lemon juice, seasoning and olive oil.

3 Scrunch up the baking parchment to make a sealed parcel and place in a shallow baking dish. Bake for 20 minutes and then serve in the paper, opening the parcel just as you are ready to eat.

Freezing not recommended

2 POINTS PER RECIPE

- **125 g (4½ oz) cod fillet**
- **2 baby leeks, trimmed and shredded lengthways**
- **finely grated zest and juice of ½ lemon**
- **½ teaspoon olive oil**
- **salt and freshly ground black pepper**

serves: **2**   preparation: **25** mins   cooking: **20** mins

5 POINTS PER RECIPE

- **250 g (9 oz) pumpkin or butternut squash, peeled, de-seeded and cut into chunks**
- **350 g (12 oz) mixed No Point root vegetables (such as swede, turnip etc.)**
- **1 garlic clove, crushed**
- **100 ml (3½ fl oz) sherry**
- **1 tablespoon cornflour**
- **1 teaspoon dried mixed herbs**
- **1 tablespoon freshly grated parmesan cheese**
- **25 g (1 oz) fresh breadcrumbs**
- **salt and freshly ground black pepper**

Autumn vegetable gratin

1 Place the pumpkin or squash, root vegetables and garlic in a large saucepan and cover with water. Bring to the boil and cook until all the vegetables are tender. Preheat the grill to medium.

2 Drain the vegetables, reserving the cooking water and place them in a flameproof dish.

3 Place 200 ml (7 fl oz) of the reserved vegetable liquid in a saucepan, add the sherry and bring to the boil. Meanwhile, add a little cold water to the cornflour and mix into a paste. Once the sherry mixture is boiling, add the paste to it and cook until slightly thickened. Add the herbs, season to taste and then pour the sauce over the vegetables.

4 Sprinkle the parmesan and breadcrumbs over the top and grill for 5–10 minutes, until browned and bubbling. This will serve two as a main course.

Freezing not recommended

Vegetable lasagne

1 Preheat the oven to Gas Mark 5/190°C/fan oven 170°C.

2 Spray a large frying pan or wok with low fat cooking spray and sauté the onion until softened. Add the courgette, peppers and mushrooms and stir fry for another couple of minutes. Pour in the pasta sauce, add the basil and season. Put to one side.

3 Using a non stick saucepan, heat all but a tablespoon of the milk. Mix the remaining cold milk with the cornflour and then add to the hot milk, stirring constantly until thickened. Season and add the mustard powder (if using). Remove from the heat and add most of the cheese, reserving some for the topping. Stir until the cheese is melted and blended.

4 Spoon half of the vegetable mixture into a shallow, large (30 x 20 cm / 8 x 12 inch) ovenproof dish. Lay half of the lasagne sheets on top, and spread about 4 tablespoons of the cheese sauce on them. Add the remaining vegetables, top with the rest of the lasagne sheets and finally the last of the cheese sauce. Sprinkle the remaining cheese over the top and bake in the oven for 40–45 minutes until bubbling and golden brown.

Freezing recommended

13½ POINTS PER RECIPE

- **low fat cooking spray**
- **1 onion, chopped**
- **1 courgette, sliced**
- **2 differently coloured peppers, de-seeded and chopped**
- **225 g (8 oz) mushrooms, sliced**
- **320 g jar of tomato pasta sauce**
- **2 teaspoons dried basil**
- **300 ml (10 fl oz) skimmed milk**
- **1½ tablespoons cornflour**
- **½ teaspoon mustard powder (optional)**
- **50 g (1¾ oz) grated half fat extra mature Cheddar cheese**
- **100 g (3½ oz) no pre cook lasagne sheets (6 sheets)**
- **salt and freshly ground black pepper**

Meatball goulash with pasta

6 ½
POINTS

26 POINTS PER RECIPE

1 Place all the meatball ingredients (except the cooking spray) in a bowl and mix thoroughly to combine. Roll small amounts of the mixture in your hands to make 20 balls.

2 Heat a large non stick frying pan and spray it with the cooking spray. Fry the meatballs in batches until brown all over and then put them to one side.

3 Add all the sauce ingredients to the pan and bring to the boil. Reduce the heat and simmer, uncovered, for 20 minutes.

4 Add the meatballs to the sauce, cover and simmer for another 10 minutes stirring occasionally. Check the seasoning.

5 Meanwhile, cook the cabbage and pasta separately in lightly salted boiling water until each is just cooked. Drain, stir together, then divide between four warmed plates. Top with the sauce and five meatballs per plate.

Freezing recommended for goulash only

- **400 g (14 oz) minced pork**
- **50 g (1¾ oz) fresh white breadcrumbs**
- **1 small onion, grated**
- **2 teaspoons paprika**
- **1 garlic clove, crushed**
- **1 egg, beaten**
- **low fat cooking spray**
- **salt and freshly ground black pepper**
  For the sauce
- **400 g can of chopped tomatoes**
- **1 tablespoon tomato purée**
- **300 ml (10 fl oz) hot chicken or vegetable stock**
- **1 teaspoon sugar**
- **1 teaspoon chopped fresh sage**
  For the pasta mixture
- **½ Savoy cabbage, shredded finely**
- **200 g (7 oz) tagliatelle**

18½ POINTS PER RECIPE

- low fat cooking spray
- **700 g (1 lb 9 oz) cooking apples, peeled, cored and quartered**
- **2 tablespoons honey**
- **50 g (1¾ oz) caster sugar**
- **1 tablespoon cornflour**
- **2 teaspoons ground cinnamon**
- **zest and juice of ½ lemon**
- **½ teaspoon vanilla essence**

  For the pastry
- **40 g (1½ oz) polyunsaturated margarine**
- **75 g (2¾ oz) plain flour plus 1 tablespoon for rolling**
- **½ teaspoon salt**
- **½ tablespoon skimmed milk**

Apple pie

1 Preheat the oven to Gas Mark 5/190°C/fan oven 170°C. Spray a 20 cm (8 inch) pie dish with the low fat cooking spray.

2 To make the pastry, mix the margarine with a tablespoon of the flour and 2 teaspoons of water. Add the rest of the flour and the salt and knead lightly until it just comes together in a ball. Put in a plastic bag in the fridge until needed.

3 Put the apples in a pan with 3 tablespoons of hot water. Cover and simmer gently for 10 minutes until the apples start to soften. Add the honey, sugar, cornflour, cinnamon, lemon zest, lemon juice and vanilla essence. Stir until thick. Leave to cool slightly.

4 Dust a work surface with the extra tablespoon of flour and roll out the pastry to fit the top of the pie dish. Put the apple mixture into the pie dish and cover with the pastry. Seal and trim the edges and pierce the pastry a few times with a fork. Decorate the top with shaped pastry trimmings if desired. Brush with the skimmed milk and bake for 30 minutes, or until the pastry is golden and crisp. Serve immediately.

Freezing recommended

Sticky banoffee puddings

18 POINTS PER RECIPE

1 Preheat the oven to Gas Mark 4/180°C/fan oven 160°C. Use the low fat cooking spray to grease four individual pudding basins (or ramekin dishes).

2 In a mixing bowl, cream together the margarine and sugar until light and fluffy. Gradually beat in the egg and stir in the vanilla extract. Sift the flour and ground ginger into the bowl, and fold in with a metal spoon. Stir in the mashed banana, dates and milk.

3 Put 1/2 tablespoon of golden syrup into the base of each basin. Top with the pudding mixture, sharing it out equally then level the surfaces.

4 Stand the basins in a roasting pan and pour in enough warm water to come halfway up their sides.

5 Bake for 30–35 minutes, until risen and golden. Run a palette knife around each pudding to release it and turn out on to a warm plate. Serve immediately.

Freezing recommended

- **low fat cooking spray**
- **50 g (1¾ oz) polyunsaturated margarine**
- **50 g (1¾ oz) light muscovado sugar**
- **1 large egg, beaten**
- **1 teaspoon vanilla extract**
- **50 g (1¾ oz) self raising white flour**
- **½ teaspoon ground ginger**
- **1 banana, mashed**
- **25 g (1 oz) dried stoned dates, chopped**
- **1 tablespoon skimmed milk**
- **2 tablespoons golden syrup**

makes: **12** slices   preparation: **10** mins + **2** hrs soaking + cooling   cooking: **50** mins

26 POINTS PER RECIPE

- **125 g (4½ oz) dried pears, chopped roughly**
- **125 g (4½ oz) dried apples, chopped roughly**
- **300 ml (10 fl oz) strong tea**
- **225 g (8 oz) plain flour**
- **2 teaspoons ground ginger**
- **2 teaspoons baking powder**
- **100 g (3½ oz) dark muscovado sugar**
- **1 egg, beaten**
- **25 g (1 oz) stem ginger, chopped**

Orchard fruit and ginger tea bread

1 Cover the dried chopped fruit with the tea and leave to soak for 2 hours. Line a 900 g (2 lb) loaf tin with greaseproof paper.

2 Preheat the oven to Gas Mark 5/190°C/fan oven 170°C. Place the dried fruit mixture, and all the remaining ingredients in a large bowl. Mix thoroughly. Spoon into the prepared tin and level the surface. Bake for 45–50 minutes until firm. (Cover with a piece of greaseproof paper during the cooking if the cake browns too quickly.)

3 Leave to cool in the tin for 10 minutes before transferring to a wire rack.

Freezing recommended

winter
recipes

serves: **4**   preparation: **10** mins   cooking: **30** mins

8 POINTS PER RECIPE

- low fat cooking spray
- **450 g (1 lb) potatoes, peeled and sliced**
- **1 large onion, sliced**
- **1.2 litres (2 pints) vegetable stock**
- **2 pinches of freshly grated nutmeg**
- **200 g (7 oz) fresh spinach**
- **2 tablespoons half fat crème fraîche**
- **salt and freshly ground black pepper**

Spinach and potato soup

1 Heat a large non stick saucepan and spray with the cooking spray. Stir fry the potatoes and onion for 1 minute. Reduce the heat to very low, season and cover the mixture with a piece of baking parchment tucked down the sides of the saucepan. Put on the saucepan lid and let the mixture 'sweat' for 20 minutes, or until soft. Shake occasionally to make sure the mixture does not stick.

2 Remove the parchment, add the stock, a couple of pinches of nutmeg and the spinach. Stir together. Bring to the boil and then liquidise or blend until smooth and check the seasoning.

3 For the best colour, immediately pour into warmed bowls and serve with $1/2$ tablespoon of crème fraîche swirled on top of each. (The lovely green of the spinach fades quite quickly.)

Freezing not recommended

Chicken broth

6 POINTS PER RECIPE

1 Heat the oil in a large saucepan and add the chicken pieces. Cook for 3–4 minutes, stirring, until sealed and browned.

2 Add all the remaining ingredients apart from the rice and bring up to the boil. Reduce the heat and simmer gently, partially covered for 20 minutes.

3 Add the rice and cook, covered, for a further 12–15 minutes, or until the rice is cooked.

4 Season to taste, then ladle into warmed bowls and serve at once.

Freezing recommended

- **1 teaspoon olive oil**
- **1 medium skinless, boneless chicken breast, chopped into small pieces**
- **1 litre (1¾ pints) hot chicken stock**
- **1 large onion, chopped finely**
- **2 carrots, diced**
- **1 small turnip, diced**
- **2 celery sticks, sliced finely**
- **2 tablespoons chopped fresh parsley**
- **50 g (1¾ oz) long grain rice**
- **salt and freshly ground black pepper**

serves: **4**   preparation: **25** mins   cooking: **2** hrs

6½ POINTS

26 POINTS PER RECIPE

- 2 teaspoons olive oil
- 500 g (1 lb 2 oz) lean braising steak, cubed
- 2 onions, sliced
- 2 celery sticks, chopped
- 2 tablespoons plain flour
- 300 ml (10 fl oz) strong dark ale
- 300 ml (10 fl oz) beef stock
- 1 bay leaf
- 1 teaspoon dried thyme
- 250 g (9 oz) mushrooms, halved
- salt and freshly ground black pepper
  For the dumplings
- 100 g (3½ oz) self raising flour
- a pinch of salt
- 1 teaspoon mustard powder
- 40 g (1½ oz) low fat spread
- 1 tablespoon finely chopped fresh chives

Beef in ale with dumplings

1 Preheat the oven to Gas Mark 3/160°C/fan oven 140°C. Heat a teaspoon of oil in a non stick, flameproof casserole dish and brown the meat all over, cooking for about 5 minutes. Remove with a slotted spoon. Add the remaining oil, the onions and celery to the pan. Cook for 5 minutes, stirring occasionally.

2 Sprinkle in the flour then gradually blend in the ale and the stock and bring to the boil. Add the bay leaf, thyme and the beef. Season, cover and cook in the oven for 1½ hours.

3 Meanwhile, make the dumplings. Sift the flour, salt and mustard into a bowl and rub in the low fat spread until the mixture resembles fine breadcrumbs. Stir in the chives and enough cold water to make a soft dough. Shape into eight small dumplings and chill until required.

4 After 1½ hours, add the mushrooms to the casserole and check the seasoning. Increase the oven temperature to Gas Mark 6/200°C/fan oven 180°C and place the dumplings on top of the casserole. Cook without the lid for another 30 minutes, or until the dumplings are crusty and golden.

Freezing recommended for casserole only

Garlic and rosemary leg of lamb

1 Rinse the lamb and pat dry. Place it in a shallow non metallic dish. Make slits all over the top of the lamb, and insert the rosemary and slices of garlic. Arrange the orange slices over the top and season well. Cover and leave to marinate for at least 3 hours, or preferably overnight.

2 Preheat the oven to Gas Mark 6/200°C/fan oven 180°C. Remove the orange slices from the lamb, move it to a roasting pan and cook for an hour. Then reduce the heat to Gas Mark 4/180°C/fan oven 160°C. Brush the lamb with the honey and cook for a further 30 minutes. Allow to stand for 15 minutes before carving.

Freezing recommended

$6\frac{1}{2}$
POINTS

25½ POINTS PER RECIPE

- **½ lean leg of lamb, approximately 1 kg (2 lb 4 oz)**
- **8 small sprigs of fresh rosemary**
- **4 garlic cloves, sliced**
- **1 orange, sliced thinly**
- **1 tablespoon clear honey**
- **salt and freshly ground black pepper**

serves: **4**   preparation: **25** mins   cooking: **55** mins

17½ POINTS PER RECIPE

- **1 onion, sliced thickly**
- **2 courgettes, sliced**
- **2 red peppers, de-seeded and cut into chunks**
- **1 aubergine, diced**
- **1 tablespoon balsamic vinegar**
- **1 tablespoon sun dried tomato purée**
- **1 teaspoon dried oregano**
- **350 g (12 oz) potatoes, peeled and sliced**
- **300 ml (10 fl oz) skimmed milk**
- **2 tablespoons cornflour**
- **100 g (3½ oz) 0% fat Greek style plain yogurt**
- **a pinch of ground nutmeg**
- **25 g (1 oz) freshly grated parmesan cheese**
- **400 g can of chopped tomatoes**
- **400 g can of borlotti beans, drained**
- **1 beef tomato, sliced**
- **salt**

Roasted vegetable moussaka

1 Preheat the oven to Gas Mark 5/190°C/fan oven 170°C and line a large baking tray with baking parchment.

2 In a large mixing bowl, toss together the onion, courgettes, peppers and aubergine with the balsamic vinegar, sun dried tomato purée, salt and oregano. Place on the baking tray and roast for 25 minutes until the vegetables are tender.

3 Cook the potatoes in a pan of lightly salted boiling water for about 7 minutes – they should be slightly undercooked at this stage.

4 Stir 3 tablespoons of the milk into the cornflour to make a paste. Heat the remaining milk and then mix in the paste. Cook until the sauce thickens. Simmer for 2 minutes, remove from the heat and stir in the yogurt, nutmeg and all but a little of the parmesan cheese. Add salt to taste.

5 When the roasted vegetables are ready, mix them with the chopped tomatoes and beans and spoon into the base of a large ovenproof dish. Arrange the potato slices over the top and spoon the sauce over them. Arrange the tomato slices over this and sprinkle the remaining parmesan on top. Bake in the oven for 30 minutes until the topping is golden and bubbling.

Freezing recommended

serves: **4**   preparation: **25** mins   cooking: **35** mins

12½ POINTS PER RECIPE

- **350 g (12 oz) baby new potatoes, halved**
- **175 g (6 oz) baby carrots, trimmed**
- **225 g (8 oz) broad beans**
- **2 leeks, sliced**
- **100 g (3½ oz) frozen peas**
- **400 g (14 oz) can of chopped tomatoes**
- **1 tablespoon dried mixed herbs**
- **2 tablespoons vermouth**
- **4 large sheets of filo pastry (50 cm x 25 cm/20 x 10 inches)**
- **25 g (1 oz) low fat spread, melted**
- **salt and freshly ground black pepper**

Vegetable pie

1 Preheat the oven to Gas Mark 6/200°C/fan oven 180°C.

2 Cook the potatoes and carrots for 10 minutes in lightly salted boiling water.

3 Add the beans, leeks and peas. Bring back to the boil and simmer for a further 5 minutes.

4 Drain the vegetables and toss with the chopped tomatoes, herbs, seasoning and vermouth. Spoon into a large ovenproof dish.

5 In turn, brush each sheet of filo pastry with the low fat spread and loosely crumple it up. Place on top of the vegetables. Arrange the pastry so that all the vegetables are covered.

6 Bake for 20 minutes, until the pastry is crisp and golden.

Freezing recommended

Tuna pasta bake

1 Preheat the oven to Gas Mark 5/190°C/fan oven 170°C. Spray a 600 ml (20 fl oz) ovenproof dish with the low fat cooking spray.

2 Cook the pasta shapes in lightly salted, boiling water according to the pack instructions. Drain well.

3 Meanwhile, cook the broccoli in lightly salted boiling water for about 6 minutes. Drain well.

4 Flake the tuna into the dish and mix in the pasta and broccoli. Beat the egg with the milk, parsley and some salt and pepper. Pour into the dish and sprinkle the cheese over the top.

5 Bake for 35–40 minutes, until set and golden.

Freezing recommended

9 POINTS PER RECIPE

- low fat cooking spray
- 100 g (3½ oz) dried pasta shapes
- 100 g (3½ oz) broccoli, cut into florets
- 200 g can of tuna in brine, drained
- 1 large egg
- 150 ml (5 fl oz) skimmed milk
- 1 tablespoon chopped fresh parsley
- 25 g (1 oz) grated half fat mature Cheddar cheese
- salt and freshly ground black pepper

serves: **4**   preparation: **30** mins   cooking: **20** mins

1½ POINTS

6½ POINTS PER RECIPE

- **low fat cooking spray**
- **1 onion, chopped finely**
- **4 garlic cloves, chopped**
- **2 celery sticks, chopped**
- **2 carrots, chopped finely**
- **400 g can of chopped tomatoes**
- **1 tablespoon chopped fresh thyme**
- **1 bay leaf**
- **250 ml (9 fl oz) fish stock**
- **finely grated zest and juice of 1 orange**
- **250 g (9 oz) haddock fillet, skinned and cut into chunks**
- **250 g (9 oz) frozen mixed seafood, defrosted**
- **salt and freshly ground black pepper**
  To garnish
- **2 red chillies, de-seeded and chopped finely (optional)**
- **chopped fresh parsley**

Italian fish stew

1 Spray a large saucepan with the cooking spray. Cook the onion, garlic, celery and carrots on a low heat for 10 minutes, or until the vegetables have softened.

2 Add the tomatoes, thyme, bay leaf, stock, orange zest and orange juice. Bring to the boil and simmer for 20 minutes, uncovered.

3 Add the haddock to the pan and cook for 3 minutes. Finally, add all the mixed seafood and cook for a further 2 minutes.

4 Season to taste and serve sprinkled with the chillies (if using) and parsley in warmed individual bowls.

Freezing not recommended

Bean and bacon brunch

1 Snip the bacon into small pieces. Spray a saucepan with the low fat cooking spray and fry the bacon with the leeks and carrot for 3–4 minutes. Then stir in the mustard, Worcestershire sauce, stock and bay leaf. Bring to the boil, cover and simmer gently for 10 minutes.

2 Remove the bay leaf, season with salt and pepper and stir in the beans. Cook for a further 2–3 minutes and serve.

Freezing not recommended

2½ POINTS PER RECIPE

- **75 g (2¾ oz) lean bacon medallions (e.g. Sainsbury's Be Good To Yourself medallions)**
- **low fat cooking spray**
- **2 baby leeks, sliced**
- **1 small carrot, chopped finely**
- **1 teaspoon wholegrain mustard**
- **½ tablespoon Worcestershire sauce**
- **75 ml (3 fl oz) chicken stock**
- **1 bay leaf**
- **100 g (3½ oz) Weight Watchers from Heinz baked beans**
- **salt and freshly ground black pepper**

Bread and butter pudding

1 Spray a 1.2 litre (2 pint) ovenproof dish with the low fat cooking spray and preheat the oven to Gas Mark 4/180°C/fan oven 160°C.

2 Lightly spread each slice of bread with the half fat butter and then the jam. Cut diagonally into triangles and layer in the dish, sprinkling a little sugar and fruit between each layer, and finishing with a layer of bread.

3 Beat the egg and the milk together and pour over the bread. Sprinkle with the cinnamon and nutmeg and, if possible, leave to stand for 30 minutes.

4 Cover with foil and bake for 45 minutes, then remove the foil. Continue to cook for 15 minutes or until just set and golden brown.

Freezing not recommended

3 POINTS

17½ POINTS PER RECIPE

- **low fat cooking spray**
- **6 medium slices of white bread**
- **40 g (1½ oz) half fat butter**
- **2 tablespoons reduced sugar apricot jam**
- **25 g (1 oz) golden caster sugar**
- **50 g (1¾ oz) raisins or sultanas**
- **1 egg**
- **600 ml (20 fl oz) skimmed milk**
- **¼ teaspoon ground cinnamon**
- **a pinch of freshly grated nutmeg, to taste**

serves: **4**   preparation: **10** mins   cooking: **20** mins

15 POINTS PER RECIPE

- **4 firm pears**
- **300 ml (10 fl oz) cranberry juice drink**
- **300 ml (10 fl oz) red wine**
- **1 cinnamon stick**
- **6 cloves**
- **2 star anise (optional)**
- **50 g (1¾ oz) dark muscovado sugar**
- **4 tablespoons low fat soft cheese**
- **4 kumquats, halved, to garnish**

Pears in mulled wine

1 Peel the pears, leaving the stalks intact. Put the pears in a saucepan with the cranberry juice, red wine, cinnamon stick, cloves, star anise (if using) and all but 4 teaspoons of the sugar. Heat gently until simmering and then cook for 15–20 minutes or until the pears are tender. Leave to cool slightly.

2 Slice the pears in half and remove the cores with a melon baller or grapefruit knife. Mix the soft cheese with 2 teaspoons of the remaining sugar. Spoon into the pear halves and arrange on serving plates.

3 Sprinkle the remaining 2 teaspoons of sugar over the top and spoon some of the red wine liquid on to the plates. Decorate with the kumquats and serve warm or cold.

Freezing not recommended

Christmas pudding and brandy sauce

53 POINTS PER RECIPE

- **low fat cooking spray**
- **100 g (3½ oz) plain flour**
- **1 teaspoon baking powder**
- **100 g (3½ oz) polyunsaturated margarine**
- **150 g (5½ oz) raisins**
- **150 g (5½ oz) sultanas**
- **100 g (3½ oz) dried apricots, chopped**
- **100 g (3½ oz) caster sugar**
- **100 g (3½ oz) fresh breadcrumbs**
- **1 teaspoon ground cinnamon**
- **1 teaspoon ground ginger**
- **½ teaspoon ground cloves**
- **1 egg, beaten**
- **150 ml (5 fl oz) skimmed milk**
- **2 tablespoons brandy**
- **40 g (1½ oz) cornflour**
- **50 g (1¾ oz) dark brown sugar**
- **600 ml (20 fl oz) skimmed milk**
- **2 tablespoons brandy**

1 Spray a 1.2 litre (2 pint) pudding basin with the low fat cooking spray and line the base with a disc of greaseproof paper. Sift the flour and baking powder into a large mixing bowl, add the margarine and rub in with your fingertips.

2 Stir in the fruit, sugar, breadcrumbs and spices. Then mix in the egg, milk and brandy. Spoon into the basin and level the surface.

3 Cover with a double thickness of greaseproof paper with a pleat in the middle to allow for rising, and tie firmly with string. Place in a steamer (or large saucepan with a tight fitting lid) one quarter full of boiling water and steam for 4½ hours. Turn out on to a serving plate.

4 To make the sauce, blend the cornflour with the sugar and a little of the milk to make a paste. Heat the rest of the milk, then mix with the paste and cook until the sugar has dissolved and the sauce has thickened, stirring constantly. Continue stirring for 2 minutes, then add the brandy and serve.

Freezing not recommended

29½ POINTS PER RECIPE

- 150 g (5½ oz) All Bran
- 200 ml (7 fl oz) skimmed milk
- 100 g (3½ oz) fructose
- 1 egg, beaten
- 100 g (3½ oz) ready to eat dried figs, chopped
- 2 small bananas, mashed
- 1 teaspoon ground nutmeg
- 50 g (1¾ oz) sultanas
- 175 g (6 oz) self raising flour

Banana and fig loaf

1 Place the All Bran in a bowl and pour over the milk. Stir and leave to stand for 20 minutes.

2 Preheat the oven to Gas Mark 4/180°C/fan oven 160°C. Line a 450 g (1 lb) loaf tin with baking parchment.

3 Stir the fructose, egg, figs, bananas, nutmeg, sultanas and flour into the All Bran mixture.

4 Spoon into the prepared tin, level the top and bake for 50 minutes to an hour, until firm to the touch. Leave to cool in the tin for a while and then transfer to a wire rack. Allow to cool completely before removing the baking parchment and cutting into slices.

Freezing not recommended